Turn, Turn, Turn

The View from a Baby Boomer's Front Porch

Jenny McLeod Carlisle

Ecclesiastes 3:1-8

To everything *there is* a season,
A time for every purpose under heaven:
A time to be born,
And a time to die;
A time to plant,
And a time to pluck *what is* planted;
A time to kill,
And a time to heal;
A time to break down,
And a time to build up;
A time to weep,
And a time to laugh;
A time to mourn,
And a time to dance;
A time to cast away stones,
And a time to gather stones;
A time to embrace,
And a time to refrain from embracing;
A time to gain,
And a time to lose;
A time to keep,
And a time to throw away;
A time to tear,
And a time to sew;
A time to keep silence,
And a time to speak;
A time to love,
And a time to hate;
A time of war,
And a time of peace.

DEDICATION

Dedicated first and foremost to our Lord and Savior Jesus Christ. As Matthew 6:33 (KJV) expresses it: "But seek ye first the kingdom of God and his righteousness; and all these things shall be added unto you." Oh, how He has added so many glorious things to my life.

To my husband, James, in gratitude for enduring my border-line insanity over all these years. The stories in my head won't leave me alone, but the best one was the dream I had as a young girl of finding the perfect man to love me and help build the family I wanted. God was so good to put me in your path at Bryant High School all those years ago. You will never fully understand how much I love you.

To John Archibald, publisher of *Ouachita Life Magazine*. When you asked me to provide the female baby boomer's perspective to your fledgling publication, who knew how we would both grow.

To my amazing kids and grands: Chris and Kat, Jon and Gina, Carrie and Chris, Jordan, Austin, Audrey, Isaac, Graham, and Foster. Here are some examples of the crazy way Mom/Granny's mind works. Intended as both insight and warning. I could just hug all of you into little bitty pieces!

CONTENTS

A Season for Reflection

A Season for Relaunching

ACKNOWLEDGMENTS

A writer's journey is never intended to be solitary. Over the years, many wonderful people and groups have encouraged me to continue.

This book in particular, though, would not exist without the help of Britta Ann Meadows (Peas in a Pod Editing and Design). So glad I ran into her and her mom in my hometown of Pittsburg, Kansas! Another God thing, for sure.

FOREWORD

Ouachita Life Magazine is a unique publication in the southwest quarter of Arkansas. Part newspaper, part magazine, it provides interesting stories about the history of the region, as well as great ideas for fun activities. My friend, John Archibald, is the editor, publisher, chief photographer, star reporter, and director of marketing and advertising. He has built a loyal following of readers who look forward to finding the free magazine at their local restaurant, chamber of commerce, or doctor's office.

We first met John when he was the district executive for our local Boy Scout Council. Always enthusiastic, he easily convinced me to send him a monthly column appealing to the active lifestyle of local baby boomers.

What a joy it has been to come up with an idea and turn it into an article that others might enjoy. Even better, meeting someone when I am out and about who says, "I really enjoy reading your stories every month."

To God be the glory!

A Season for Rebirth

The New Year always provides a new chance…new dreams. For a few days, our record is unbroken: no disappointments, at least not yet. In Arkansas, though, it can be a volatile time. The weather can go from winter to spring and back again, with ice storms and severe thunderstorms sometimes happening in the same week.

The birth of a year, just like the birth of a child, is promising, but never boring or easy.

On the Threshold —
You Can Go Either Way

I have always loved front porches. You can ask my husband and children. If Granny comes up missing, look to the rocker just outside the door. When the weather is nice, I may take a book and a cup of tea out there, but even during a thunderstorm, it's the perfect spot to stay in touch with what's happening in the real world. There's just enough shelter to protect me from the elements, and a couple of quick steps brings me back to the safety of the house.

At the beginning of a new year, we think a lot about entrances…beginnings. The old custom of a groom carrying his bride across the threshold is a classic symbol of a fresh start. From what I can glean from my research, the threshold originated as a board inside the door of the house. Apparently, the refuse from processing (threshing) grain was used on the earthen floors to keep them from becoming a muddy mess. Carrying the bride not only protected her from tripping, but also from sullying her pretty shoes and wedding dress. It was one more way for her new husband to show his deference and concern.

Some of my fondest memories have to do with beginnings. I can recall minute details of the day we got married, the day each of our children was born, the day we moved into our new house. Maybe the reason those memories stick is because our emotions were at their peak. There was a little bit of fear and uncertainty mixed with jubilation and pride. It was exhilarating to be in that place of imminent change. As each milestone passed and new became ordinary, the next experience or challenge waited in the wings, and the excitement returned.

The view from my rocker is reminiscent of my growing-up years. Kids riding bikes and skating on the sidewalks, moms and dads unloading groceries, the neighborhood cat making his rounds. I feel almost invisible as I observe, peacefully soaking it all in. A recent country song takes a different angle, as the writer explains "the view I love the most is from my front porch looking in."

As 2009 begins, we get a chance to start anew. We can stop at the threshold for just a moment and look back. Most likely, there are both good and bad memories from the past year. Many things probably didn't turn out as we expected. But, looking ahead, we can gather strength from what we've learned, and valiantly step over.

From my in-laws' front porch, you look directly out at Thornburg Mountain. It's amazing to consider the beauty of God's creation, and we are so grateful to have such wonderful vistas close by. But, to experience the beauty of nature, we must venture out occasionally. Feel the breeze on our faces, listen to the blessed silence. Don't be afraid this year to get out and enjoy the amazing sights and activities available in the Ouachita area. When you're home again, take a deep breath and relax. If you don't have a porch of your own, check this space each month. I plan to be right here, sharing the view from mine, and looking forward to crossing that next threshold.

2017: Uncharted Waters

When we were younger, the arrival of a new year was all about the celebration. When I was still in high school, our local movie theater sponsored an *American Graffiti* marathon on New Year's Eve. That was also the year of a huge ice storm in my Southeast Kansas hometown. So, after watching the inspiration for the *Happy Days* TV series four or five times, we ventured out into the icy streets. My boyfriend's mom had some treats prepared at his house, and instead of asking our parents to drive on the glassy pavement, we decided to walk (slide) the several blocks from the main drag. Another friend showed up with bottle rockets, which whizzed down the empty streets for what seemed like miles. An exciting, explosive celebration for sure!

After a move to Arkansas, and finding the right man to marry, the New Year's celebrations continued. When our kids were small, we took advantage of willing grandparents for overnight visits and tried out some area restaurants for some special nights out. Then, as the youngsters got older, we challenged them to stay up until the ball dropped, consuming lots of frozen pizza and cheese dip at home.

When our nest began to empty, hubby and I ventured across the country for a visit with some friends who had moved to the East Coast. Arriving at the airport just before midnight, we welcomed the new year in a Waffle House between Baltimore and Washington. On that same trip, we enjoyed a brunch cruise on the Potomac. Great scenery, and memories to last a lifetime.

Somewhere along the way, the turning of the calendar

page became less about the party and more about what the new year might bring. We looked back on varying levels of our kids' education, and forward to what it would take to finish. Significant others came into the family, and talk of weddings, and then grandbabies, filled up our calendars and our New Year's Eve brains. New countdowns emerged as we realized that long-scheduled retirement benefits might actually be within reach, and we plotted the last day of our long-held jobs, along with what might happen afterwards.

Dick Clark, the poster child for the Peter Pan dream of never growing old, did exactly that, and after a last display of bravery, gave his seat in Times Square over to Ryan Seacrest. The world would never be the same.

So, this year, along with the rest of the "last gasp" baby boomers, our ages will begin with the numeral six. A strange place to be. Just yesterday, we were putting on our new P.F. Flyers and zooming up and down on our Christmas bicycles, with their banana seats and butterfly handlebars. These days, we spend much more time in our recliners, saving our strength for the nine-to-five routines that we just can't let go of yet.

Once again, we are too busy looking forward to spend much time glancing back. For a few days in the first month of the year, we will be cruising in the warm Caribbean sun while most of you are shivering in the Ouachita winter weather. Before too long, we plan to return to Florida to meet our sixth grandbaby. There will most likely be a week devoted to "Granny Camp", when we gather as many of the kids as possible for some wonderful chaos. The oldest grandson is now a musician, so we hope to be in the audience for some of his concerts and competitions. These coming events promise to be ten times more exciting than any one-night celebration.

From past experience, we know that there will be some surprises, some setbacks along the way. But, rather than dreading these things, we can take them in stride. There is very little that life can throw our way that can't be handled with a little extra prayer.

This year, I hope you find happiness in your own life as you continue to enjoy my rambling thoughts. If you are so inclined, drop me a line in care of *Ouachita Life*. It helps a writer to know that someone is out there reading and reacting. There is no way to know what the voyage into 2017 will bring, but won't it be fun to embark together!

Life After the Glass Slipper

As a new year dawns, we wonder what it will hold in store. New beginnings always get our hearts racing a little bit, especially if we know that some milestone in our lives is about to occur. Weddings, graduations, and new houses all hold a shining promise as we anticipate how wonderful our lives could become.

But even Cinderella must have had some modifications to make during her "happily ever after." After all, she was a common servant girl who suddenly became the focus of attention, with attendants of her own to fulfill her every desire. Now, instead of "Cinderella, scrub this, Cinderella, sweep that," she would hear, "No, Your Majesty, let me do that. Please, Your Majesty, sit down and relax." It's a problem we would all like to experience just once, but an adjustment just the same.

When I was a small child, I dreamed of having a full-time daddy living in our house. My parents were divorced, and I enjoyed the summer vacations with my dad and his new wife, but I longed for what I considered to be a "complete" family. When, in my teens, my mom met and began dating my future stepdad, it was literally a dream come true. When they married, it started the biggest change I'd ever lived through. My sister and I suddenly had a new house in a new state, and a new school along with our new family. The high school was smaller than our old one, and all of the kids tried hard to make us feel at home. But, what an adventure! It was much more than I had bargained for in my little-girl fantasies.

Of course, my dreams continued, and I pictured in my mind what my own happy family would look like. Led by a strong, Christian man, with two, or even three, beautiful children, I would fit right in, caring for all of them with love and occasional home-baked cookies.

When a certain tall, smooth-talking Arkansas boy entered my life, I knew this dream, too, was on its way to being fulfilled. His upbringing provided the perfect example of the stability I was longing for, and besides, he was really cute! So, after a simply beautiful wedding with a wonderful assortment of family and friends in attendance, we settled into our first home: a rented single-wide trailer decorated in hip seventies' fashion with wood paneling and harvest-gold and avocado-green appliances. We soon learned that in order to afford the things we wanted, we would need to hold down two full-time jobs. So, after a couple of false starts apiece, we both settled into what would become careers and began the daily commutes. The three beautiful children arrived on schedule, each with their own set of happy adjustments to make in our fairy tale.

Along the way, we realized that our careers would have advanced further if we had a little more education, but this idea was quickly pushed to the back burner in the daily rush of coats and mittens and sack lunches for five. Opportunities abounded and we became involved in the activities of our own children, and along the way had the chance to impact others in our community as well. The old dreams morphed and developed into more excitement than we ever envisioned.

These days, the kids are all successfully independent, and our empty nest is still buzzing, especially when the grandkids visit. We couldn't have written a happier ending if we'd tried.

This year, another long-awaited event looms. Over the years, I was promised that even though my job did not include a huge salary, if I stayed around long enough, I could retire at a fairly early age and enjoy the rewards of working through a lot of headaches. This little dream has had plenty of time to develop, and it mostly stars me at this computer: creating, editing, and submitting for publication the stories that have buzzed through my head for well over fifty years. Surprise! The glass slipper comes with some complications. Because of recent economic downturns, my husband and I are both looking for new jobs to either accommodate the lifestyle we've worked so hard to build, or trim it down a little. We are both hopeful, yet becoming used to the feeling of butterflies in our stomachs once again. Hmmm—if all else fails, maybe we can find another two-bedroom trailer, this time with a workshop for him, and a wireless internet connection for me. Hold our hands, Lord. This year will undoubtedly turn out far differently than we ever could have dreamed!

How You Know It's for Real— Hindsight is Always Best

Young people seem to have a common concern: How can I be sure that this person is right for me? The most oft-repeated response: You just know.

Looking back, there were plenty of indications that this guy was different. For one, there were the notes he wrote me at school. I'd written plenty of giggly missives in my time, and received plenty back. But notes exchanged between teenage girls are mainly time-wasters. Much like doodling with words. There was a lot of "so and so just looked at me" and "don't you think he's cute?" Very much the same as teenaged telephone conversations, except without the polite pauses to see what the other person should say. The notes from this guy, however, were very sweet, complimentary, and thoughtful. The kind that make you go "awwwww."

We really enjoyed each other's company, and loved hanging out, with or without a group of mutual friends. When he took the big step of taking me to meet his family, it seemed they were instantly sure of the "rightness" of the relationship. One Sunday afternoon, we sat in lawn chairs just to the east of Thornburg Mountain with his parents and grandparents. During a short lull in the conversation, his grandpa, who was literally a man of few words, piped up with, "When are y'all gettin' married?" A few minutes later, as a storm crept over the top of the mountain, his grandma whispered to me, "Let's go inside; the rest of them can get wet if they want to." I was in.

My own magic moment is etched in my memory. I don't recall what kind of date we were coming home from. It could have been the latest Burt Reynolds movie, or a sausage, pepperoni, and mushroom pizza at Ken's on Military Road in Benton, or maybe both. We were riding in his dad's pickup because he had wrecked his car on the way to pick me up for a previous date. He looked straight ahead as I slid in as close as possible while still allowing him to drive, and soon came out with a confession. He said he couldn't imagine the rest of his life without me in it. I couldn't believe he said it, and I couldn't have agreed more. No ring, so the real proposal came later, but, from that moment, happily ever after was a foregone conclusion for me.

Thirty-five and a half years later, those first indications proved to be right on. He was the husband and father I had dreamed of since I was a very small girl. Yin to my yang, he balanced my creativity and impulsiveness with his desire for perfection and certainty.

Raising three kids was never easy, but, together, we found the fun. We laughed and cried together, and now we stand back and smile as three happy little families form the next tier of our family tree.

We're blessed with good friends that we've met and held on to over the years. When we spend time with those folks, I can hear the story he's about to share before he gets it started, and we fill in the blanks for each other. I'm so fortunate to have my best friend to go home with when all is said and done. With him, I can be me, and he's learned to put up with my annoying habits and contrary ways. I thank God daily for this amazing gift.

Valentine's Day is set aside to celebrate the loving relationships in our lives. If you're not in the middle of one right now, I hope you have happy memories to look back on, and a good outlook that will lead to something wonderful in your future. Regardless, my fervent prayer is that you'll recognize and appreciate the unconditional love of your Heavenly Father on Valentine's Day and every day.

Neither Rain, Nor Sleet, Nor Snow ... Well, Maybe ...

In the words (loosely translated) of an old poet: "The best laid schemes of mice and men quite often go awry." Around here, the most common reason for that derailment is the unpredictability of the Arkansas weather.

This winter, we almost literally held our breath through December and January. In spite of a few days with some seriously cold temperatures, the precipitation associated with after-Christmas bargain hunting and white sales stayed largely to our north and east. We just knew that at any point, the other snow boot could drop, and we'd be in for a white February.

Sure enough, many parts of our region got pounded by an icy blast, leaving slick streets and stranded motorists in its wake. Even though we had been lucky to that point, by the end of the week after Valentine's Day, we had had enough, and were eagerly awaiting the arrival of the daffodils. It's not that we hate winter; it's just that it can be so doggoned inconvenient. Many of us would have been glad to work, if we could get our vehicles out of our driveways. Staying home and enjoying a hot cup of cocoa became the only option.

Winter is not the only season when Mother Nature can foil our plans. We have all learned to have at least one alternative ready, no matter how long we have looked forward to an outdoor activity.

As a high school band student, one of the biggest honors is to be selected to be your state's representative in the Cherry

Blossom Festival parade in Washington, DC. My group, from a small Kansas town about the size of Arkadelphia, raised funds for well over a year for our fifteen minutes of fame. We boarded buses on our spring break from school and made the twenty-seven-hour trip, eager to show that the early morning and long after-school practices would pay off. On the day of the big parade, the rain came down in *torrents*. Faced with the idea of going home without performing, our band booster parents came up with a solution to help protect our brand-new uniforms and expensive instruments. The improvisation gave us a new name: The Marching Garbage Bags. Undaunted, we played our hearts out, and finally broke ranks at the end of the route to run to the safety of the buses.

Another youthful adventure that seems to always break a drought is a camping trip. One hot summer, during my third year of Girl Scout summer camp, I participated in an excursion called wilderness camp. The plan was that we would carve a campsite out of an undeveloped spot in the woods, clear a place to cook safely, dig our own bathroom facility, and sleep in hammocks, instead of tents. Digging in the rain was not too bad, cooking under a tarp was bearable, but, oh, the misery of zipping a sleeping bag over my head and swinging from dripping tree branches at night. No one could have planned a better character building exercise than that one.

I recalled that time many years later when I volunteered with our sons' scout troop. This time, sleeping was done in nice, dry tents. The highlight of the weekend was a competition where the boys were to construct camp furniture by lashing sticks together. Our troop had practiced at home, and knew exactly what they wanted to do. After their surprise that there was no cancellation due to the heavy downpour, I witnessed a minor miracle. I remember the pure joy on their faces as they looked around and realized that all of the other teams were operating under the same situation. How did they deal with it? By pitching in, working as a team, and laughing all the way. The one thing I don't recall about that contest is who received the prize. I think we all won that day.

Last year, our family was very happy to attend the wedding of a couple who was dear to all of our hearts. Both had been married before, but were certain that this time the golden bands would be on the right left hands. The ceremony was to be held in a pavilion in the city park, with informality and simple beauty the theme of the day. Surely, we thought, even a little shower wouldn't hurt, since the pavilion was large enough to accommodate all of the guests that were expected. That day, though, there was more than a little shower. The grounds around the covered picnic spot were soaked and muddy, and there was no sign that the sun would appear at all, even for a short time. So, an emergency move to a very gracious church fellowship hall saved the day, and provided a terrific place for eating and visiting afterwards. Dry and happy smiles dominate the wedding pictures, and the day could not have been more perfect.

The moral of these stories? Be prepared, but prepare to be unprepared. Sometimes, the worst-laid plans may be the best, after all.

When the Past Meets the Future

Last Friday, I ate my lunch in what used to be the service bay of a full-service gas station in Little Rock. The big sliding overhead doors remained, but inside, tables and chairs sat where the cars used to wait patiently to be repaired. Outside, big trucks were connected to power generators, the noisy roar testifying to the activity that was taking place inside. Most likely converted from another use themselves, these vehicles now house stoves, refrigerators, and one or two very busy chefs who are serving the best in portable cuisine to happy customers. Mobile food service is hardly new. But what used to be lovingly called "roach coaches" have evolved into a very trendy and new culture of fine dining.

The juxtaposition of old and new has always fascinated me. The old church building that has stood through centuries of progress in the same spot as modern new buildings crowded in from all sides. The sign in front of a business that was never taken down when new owners converted the space to a new use. A living history presentation where the presenters are totally in character as visitors in modern clothes snap pictures on their iPhones.

Like time capsules from the past, these treasures connect us to the folks who came before us. By visiting and listening, we can begin to sense what life was like for them before the modern conveniences we now take for granted had even been envisioned.

Another confession: I have always been attracted to abandoned houses. It all goes back to my love for a good story. I think that by walking through these dilapidated structures, I will be able to hear the walls talking, sharing the laughter and tears of the families who lived there.

My mother certainly shared this interest. When my sister and I were small, we traveled to a town north of our home in Southeast Kansas, where an army facility had stood since the days of the Civil War. After the proper tour was concluded, we noticed an old house that was in the process of being torn down. Always up for an adventure, Mom led us through the rooms of peeling wallpaper and drooping plaster to an old bedroom upstairs. I remember how bright it was in this room, unencumbered by curtains, or even proper glass in the windows. Here, we found that old newspapers had been affixed to the walls. She explained that this was a common practice. Reusing the daily "rag" for added insulation was an early example of recycling. Even better, you had a chance to reread the news of days past. On one piece that was begging to be peeled off of the wall, we found a story about our local pharmacist during his glory days as a professional baseball player. She may have debated the legalities for a moment, but ultimately saved this scrap of the past from the burn pile, and took it to our friend, who was, of course, very pleased to be remembered. DISCLAIMER—I am in no way encouraging trespassing. Exploring old buildings without permission is dangerous and illegal.

Folks who are afflicted with the "talking walls" disease are also the kind who love to leave treasures for future explorers to find. Buried in the concrete of the porch my stepdad built in the mid-nineteen seventies is a Bicentennial mason jar from the Minute Man restaurant. It contains a note written by my mom describing the people who lived in our house, along with a Bicentennial quarter, and a couple of other very significant items. While we are confessing, I will admit that I have hidden a couple of similar time capsules in my present home. I refuse to give any further clues at this time, as they are certainly not worthy of anyone coming in with sledge hammers to search for them today.

Historic preservation is all about hanging on to a few things from the past that will benefit the children of the future. Not all children will care, but there are still a few out there.

On another lunch break in Little Rock recently, my grandson looked around inside the popular pizzeria.

"When was this place built?" he asked me.

"Well, I am not sure, but when we go outside, we will look to see if they posted the date somewhere. You know, I don't think it has always been a restaurant. What do you think might have been here before?" I could almost hear his wheels turning.

"They probably sold drugs," he said matter-of-factly.

"You mean, a pharmacy? With a soda fountain?" Maybe not true of this spot, but a good idea, I thought to myself.

"No. Drugs, cigarettes, stuff like that."

Hmm. Maybe they need to brighten this place up a little. The kid is thinking pretty dark thoughts about its past.

Sure enough, the date just after the turn of the twentieth century was proudly displayed in the old brick façade above the second story windows. Whether my grandson will investigate further about this particular piece of history remains to be seen. But the spark is lit. He loves to think about what happened before even his old gray-haired Granny walked the earth.

The legacy continues.

A Season for

Relaxation

There are a few days every summer when Arkansans appreciate the sunshine. A. Very. Few. Gardeners enjoy getting out and encouraging the flowers, the vegetables, or the lawn to grow. Kids chase the ice cream truck, run through the sprinklers, splash in the pool. But for most of the second quarter of the year, air conditioning is our friend. The oppressive heat and humidity cause a full retreat. Every year, I provide a reading list designed for feet up, fan on, sweet tea close at hand relaxation. But, it is, after all vacation-time. So, here's to the simple things, like digging in the garden, singing in the car, taking the grandkids to Disney. Well, not all vacations are simple.

Bloom Where You Are Planted

How did you get where you are today? No, I'm not looking for your "self-made man" stories here. I don't want to hear about the day you were discovered at the corner drugstore and became a star. I'm thinking more about the myriad of stories in your family's past that caused a change in location, bringing new opportunities, and how you've made the best of them.

This is one of my Mom's favorite angles when she researches family history. Why did a family move from Kentucky to California? Just look at the future generations it affected. In our family's case, if my great-grandmother had not moved herself and two small children that incredible distance to live near a brother who had already settled there, my grandfather and grandmother would never have met. My grandmother was there because her parents, both of German descent, had retired from the military at the Presidio. So, how in the world did I end up in Arkansas? That takes several more stories.

Perhaps even more telling, though, is what happens next. How do the children adapt and adjust when they are uprooted and replanted?

It must have been a huge culture shock for my mom when she moved from the San Francisco Bay Area as a teenager to a farm in South Central Kansas. But, she says she loved the sunshine and working outdoors. At the small town school she attended, she flourished, and was elected President of the Student Body before she graduated. No small feat for a girl in post-WWII America.

43

In my job with the State of Arkansas, I've been privileged to work with people from Asia, South Africa, and Eastern Europe. How difficult it must be to adapt to a country with strange customs and a language that makes very little sense. Remarkably, many of these people speak better English than I do, though you must listen carefully at times to communicate well.

Once, my friend Kristina had a new chair in her office with the tag still attached. As I helped her remove it, I introduced her to Minnie Pearl, a legendary American icon remembered for the price tags that dangled from her hats. Imagine how strange that story must be to someone who's never seen the Grand Ole Opry. But, there's another example of someone who thrived in her environment. Miss Minnie was a great lady, both onstage, with her hilarious antics, and off, where Sarah Cannon was an incredible force for good in the Nashville community.

Sometimes, it's not the choices our family makes, but our own that change our situation. When I was a little girl, I had two dreams. One was of a happy family with a mommy, daddy, and two or three kids. The other was to write stories. Very early, I found out that writing stories might not pay much, so I aimed at being a teacher and writing stories on the side. Little did I know that the happy family dream would come first, putting the teaching and writing goals on hold. But today I have three kids and four really grand kids, and I'm still in love with their really grand daddy. At work, I teach people to use computers…and the writing? It's coming along. It took a little while, and a much different route than I had anticipated, but hey, I'm blooming in my own way.

You still want to hear how our family tree made it from Kansas to Arkansas, and now has branches in Texas and Florida? Good. That means I still have stories to write. As springtime comes to the Ouachitas, enjoy your family gardens, wherever they may be planted.

What's the Matter with Kids Today?

One of the many songs that runs through my brain on a regular basis starts out this way: "Kids! I don't know what's wrong with these kids today!" It goes on to complain about the strange way the younger generation talks, the weird things that interest them. The plea of the song is summed up like this: "Why can't they be like we were, perfect in every way? What's the matter with kids today?" Sound familiar? Do you hear folks expressing this thought quite often these days? Remember, this song was written in 1960 for the Broadway musical *Bye, Bye Birdie.*

Looking back, my own generation was certainly not perfect. In the late sixties and early seventies, our parents stressed over the music we listened to. Far worse than that was the drug culture that permeated everything. In fact, given all the dangerous things we did as teenagers, we are very fortunate to have lived long enough to be grandparents.

So, are kids really any worse than we were? No, just different. And who exactly are we referring to here? As my own offspring grow up, the top age limit is creeping into the mid-thirties now.

Social networking is their cup of tea, and they use it to full advantage. One of my friends on Facebook is not even human; it's a Van. With some human assistance from a young visionary and many like-minded folks, the Van delivers necessities like shoes, socks, and toiletries to the homeless population of Central Arkansas. Now, the Van even pulls a converted trailer, which houses a portable shower. In my daily walk from my car to my high-rise office, the people I encounter are starting to look cleaner and happier.

This generation also loves to mobilize and act quickly. When one of them has a problem, they create prayer pages and fund-raising pages that get hundreds of hits each day. Community events like car washes, pancake fundraisers, mass races and "walks" kick into high gear. One local police officer, who we met before he became an Eagle Scout, recently went on television to have his head shaved in support of a fellow officer's young child who has cancer.

The baby boomers were raised in front of the TV set. Our children substituted video games for television programs. We worried, thinking that the games were robbing our children of the ability to think for themselves. Quite the contrary.

At the University of Washington, a competition called "Foldit" enticed avid gamers to help in finding a cure for HIV (AIDS). Participants worked to create a virtual model of an enzyme that the scientists had been unable to build. The originators of the game wanted to see if human intuition could succeed where automated methods have failed. When the gamers quickly solved the first puzzle, they realized that the ingenuity of game players is a formidable force.

As these gamers become the workers and executives of top companies, we find that their skills are being incorporated into their jobs. Smart companies take advantage of their imagination and creativity to find new solutions for old problems. By making tough issues into competitions, these "kids" are making amazing strides.

Of course, not all of the members of this generation are so altruistic and caring. No more than our own generation is perfect. But, in the hands of Generation X and Generation Y, I think we can feel safe. All in all, they're pretty good kids. Are we surprised? Not really. After all— look at who raised them.

Taking the Show on the Road

"Ain't she cute…See her riding down the chute…Now I ask you very confidentially…ain't she cute."

Who recorded this song? Did it sell a million records? I couldn't tell you. I only heard it when my dad was behind the wheel of his 1960s Buick.

The acoustics were better in my mom's Volkswagen Beetles, both the 1963 and the 1967 models, and the 1973 VW Fastback. Here's where we formed a family trio, Sister singing lead soprano, and Mom and I providing alto and tenor harmonies. Our selections varied widely, from hymns and choir anthems, to the Beatles and even Tanya Tucker's "Delta Dawn."

My oldest son caught the bug quite early. He knew every word to Kenny Rogers' "Gambler" at the age of three. The first few times he sang "I wish you could have turned my head, and left my heart alone…", I was scrambling for a pencil, thinking I had a musical prodigy on my hands. I was just a little disappointed when I heard the Oak Ridge Boys perform the same song on the car radio, and realized that's where he'd learned it.

My daughter says that one of her favorite memories of summer vacations involve me and her dad assisting Conway Twitty and Loretta Lynn on their duets while driving. "Louisiana woman…Mississippi man.…We get together every time we can." The kids in the back seat happily provided the back-up.

The second son also took his old buddy Conway, along with other artists of all varieties, on trips back and forth to

Fayetteville. Windows rolled down, stereo turned up, plenty of Mountain Dew for energy—the trip out of the mountains seemed a little shorter.

The next generation of vocalists is thriving, too. Oldest grandson Jordan could sing recognizable melodies before he could form complete sentences. One of his favorite serenades from the back seat started with the words "my Jesus, my Savior." After that, the words he sang were not intelligible, even though the tune was intact. He was really disappointed, though, that I didn't know the words either. After several lessons from him, and a few trips around the Christian radio dial, I finally got the hang of it, and we made a pretty good team.

Latest to join the family "circle" is grandson Austin. At five, his favorites are Johnny Cash and Willie Nelson, though he also belts out "I Saw the Light" by Hank Williams (senior).

A couple of years ago, a writer friend of mine accompanied me to a conference in Southeast Kansas. We attended the early service at two different churches before starting back home that Palm Sunday. Something about the Ozark mountains must have inspired us, as we sang every hymn our memories could muster from the top of "the hill" in Fayetteville to well past Morrilton on I-40. Though we knew many of the same songs, she taught me some new verses, and I expanded her repertoire with my old-time Church of Christ selections.

So, the logical end of this story would be that at least one family member or friend now lives in Nashville, and a recording career looms on the horizon. Sorry to disappoint you, but hey—none of us has ever been arrested for road rage, either! Enjoy the rest of your summer, and if you see me tooling down the freeway with my mouth wide open in song, just wave!

Leave the Island and Find Your Tribe

It's right there in the first book of the Bible: "And God said, 'It is not good that man should be alone.'" Of course, there are times when we want peace and quiet and solitude, but to be happy and healthy, we need contact with others. In other words, if you're going to be stranded on an island, hang out with Gilligan, rather than Tom Hanks and his volleyball. Sharing an interest with others also means learning to speak their language.

When hubby and I were dating, I wanted to be able to talk to him about the things he was interested in. It was not really too hard for me to learn to speak "car." My first real job out of high school was at the switchboard of a new car dealership. After my college classes were over for the day, I spent a few hours in front of the huge plate glass windows, watching the passing traffic. There were not a lot of phone calls coming in after 5 o'clock. I made a game out of trying to guess what model of vehicle was approaching, by the configuration of their headlights. The salesmen that worked there helped too, as knowledge of all things automotive was literally their bread and butter.

My Prince Charming cheerfully accommodated me, as well. There were lots of things to learn, I am sure. If I wished that one of my friends would "break a leg" I really meant them no harm. This came from the school plays and summer theater productions I had been involved in. Actors, like athletes, are a superstitious lot. To guarantee that a performance would go well, there were rituals and traditions to be maintained. Before each show, we would gather for a short "pep talk" that always included an odd ceremony. Since I've not been in the habit for a long time, the details escape me, but I remember it involved standing in a circle holding hands and hopping on one foot. The "break a leg" thing was actually a form of reverse psychology. Wishing someone good luck would cause some catastrophe to occur. When I hear of an accident happening onstage, I always wonder if these actors skipped the "circle time" that night, or heaven forbid, someone yelled "good luck" just before they ran out of the wings.

We did share several things in common, as all good couples do. We both had a love of music, so driving around with the stereo cranked up was a perfectly acceptable date night for us. We both became very good at "Name That Tune" and would often challenge each other to guess the artist of a song we heard on the radio. As children were added to the back seat, they tolerated our duets and became our biggest fans. Though I was born in Kansas, and he hailed from right here in Central Arkansas, we can belt out "Louisiana Woman, Mississippi Man" almost as well as Conway and Loretta did.

Not every aspect of my husband's life came so naturally to me. He loves working with wood and building useful and beautiful furniture. I have listened as he extolled the virtues of one power tool over another and watched hours of television programs where the main objective is to transform a mediocre or inconvenient room to a modern and practical showplace. I put up with hours of watching a sink being installed so that when something slips or breaks in our own castle, the "king" will know what to do, or at the very least, who to call. The only drawback to this interest of his is that my car barely fits in the garage, which is now doubling for a well-stocked workshop.

The major leap for him, I know, has been to adjust to my love for reading and writing. He has grown used to seeing my nose in a book, and weathered the addition of reading glasses and the flickering light of my Kindle reader. He endures my constant chatter about agents and publishers, and even my need to run off for long weekends of workshops and writing retreats. Some evenings, he wishes I would be sitting next to him, learning about his latest DIY project, instead of retreating to this keyboard to tap away on the story that won't let me go. But, after years of togetherness, we have both adjusted.

Last weekend, I quietly walked away as he conversed with a fellow woodworker, deciding on which new tool to add to his arsenal. This week he gamely accompanied me as I soaked in the beauty of a Shakespearean play. We both understand that, just like on the old TV show, "sometimes you want to go where everybody knows your name."

What I Learned on My Summer Vacation

What a summer this has been for the Carlisle family. It was definitely one for the record books. Before we dig out the sweatshirts and start adding pumpkin spice to everything, let's take a good deep breath and look back. There were lots of valuable lessons to be learned.

1. Train up your children in the way they should go, and when you have your fortieth wedding anniversary, they just might throw you a really nice party. We had lots of friends in our church fellowship hall on a stormy Sunday afternoon. A beautiful cake, lots of hugs, and even a declaration of congratulations from the county judge. Not half shabby! Instead of gifts, our family and friends presented us with some cash to be used towards a future cruise.

2. Cousins have a natural love for each other. They just need opportunities to spend time together. Our five live in three different states, but within a few minutes of reuniting, they have the very best time. Playing, laughing, scheming together. What a joy. Noisy, tiring, but wonderful.

3. Disney really has this magical vacation thing down to a science. We were amazed at how every detail of our vacation came together. From just the right lodging at their resort, transportation from the airport and all around their property, to cooking s'mores at a campfire

sing-along. They thought of everything. There is so much more to Disney than movies and amusement park rides. There are a lot of great places to take your kids and grandkids, but everyone ought to have at least one Disney adventure.

4. Helping people feels good. After returning from our vacation, it was a real joy to help with the annual backpack distribution at Ralph Bunche Park in Benton. Our community really turned out to offer services of all kinds to get these kids and their parents off to school on the right foot. Another hot, steamy day, but one that was filled with smiles.

5. A tropical storm can wreak havoc even if it doesn't have a name. The same storm that displaced so many of our Louisiana neighbors in August seemed to just sit on Central Arkansas for weeks. Because it was annoying, and very persistent, I suggested that we call it Tropical Storm Dennis the Menace. Though the rain was not extremely heavy here, it was continuous. We became accustomed to carrying umbrellas, dashing to our cars, splashing through puddles. The upside of this was that our grass, our crepe myrtles, and the more tropical plants like elephant ears were greener and prettier than they have been in years. We learned the literal meaning of making hay while the sun shines. The window for mowing lawns was short, so they looked shaggy quite often. So different from the parched, drought-stricken Augusts we have come to expect.

6. It's not hard to find some very well-organized

community-minded organizations in the Ouachita region. I attended the thirtieth anniversary celebration of the Saline County History and Heritage Society and heard stories of how they had grown and persevered over the years. From their permanent location in downtown Benton, they continue to document and share valuable information. More recently, I visited with a very well-organized group of women (and one brave gentleman) at the Garland County Extension Homemakers Summer Council Meeting. Resourceful, happy, and dedicated to encouraging each other; it was inspiring to see how they keep their many projects thriving. This made me eager to rededicate myself to the groups I am involved with.

7. A full calendar gives us hope for the future. Right now, I am looking forward to a fund-raising yard sale for a historical preservation group, a retreat with a group of writers, a trip with my husband to a professional football game, and, sometime after the holidays, that exciting cruise! With so many things to plan for, there is no time for fretting or worrying. Much too busy for that.

I hope that all of you had a very good summer, and are now looking forward to the glorious Arkansas autumn. I would love to hear about the lessons you have learned. Send your letters in care of Ouachita Life, or find me on Facebook!

A Season for Rejuvenation

I would like to see statistics on this: How many people who first visit Arkansas in the autumn eventually move there permanently? The humidity goes away, the tornadoes leave us alone, and thousands of folks gather for football, marching band competitions, and festivals of all types. Sunshine, autumn colors, camp-fires…Ahhh. It doesn't get any better than this. It never seems to last long enough.

Ouachita Autumn— A Glorious Sigh of Relief

Granny Autumn is spreading this year's version of her patchwork quilt across our favorite hills and valleys. Each day she adds a new swatch of bright crimson, bold yellow, or flaming orange, while always leaving just enough pine green for contrast. Tucked in some of the most unlikely places, a blazing display amazes us, prompting a quick deep breath of clean, fresh fall air.

Low humidity and cool morning breezes make for perfect opened-sunroof weather. Accompanied by our favorite traveling music, even the dreaded commute to work is easier to endure.

Weekends are packed to overflowing with opportunities for family fun. We can choose from community festivals, charity races, contests, and exhibits of all kinds.

High school and college football games are like living time capsules. We close our eyes and we're transported several decades back. The same songs played by the band, the same shouts by enthusiastic young voices fill our ears. The smells of concession stand foods still tempt us. Opening our eyes, there are many sights that haven't changed much over the years. Homecoming royalty still walk out onto the football field in dresses and shoes that were never meant for the outside. Cheerleaders attempt daring jumps while their mothers cringe. Players jump impatiently along the sidelines. Coaches still shake their heads as they try to hold their tempers.

Even working in our own yards is enjoyable. We can get more accomplished because it just feels so great to be out there. Flowerbeds overflow with bales of hay and chrysanthemums. Displays are easily converted from Halloween to Thanksgiving by removing spider webs and jack-o'-lanterns and adding a pilgrim or two.

We enjoy wearing jackets and sweatshirts, but not because they're vital for survival. They just feel good and look great.

Soon enough, cool temperatures and sunshine will give way to cloudy, cold winter. But, by then, we will have our pansies planted, so we'll still have some bright colors to cheer us.

We should all enjoy each day of this season before the holidays occupy our thoughts. It's a time when simple pleasures are the best, and we remember why we love living here.

A little unfinished business from October: By the time you read this, another very active community organization will have held a worthwhile event in Benton. CJCOHN (Churches Joint Council on Human Needs) sponsored a coat drive to outfit all ages and sizes with warm outerwear for the upcoming winter. Thanks to Arkansas Prosthetics and Pedorthics and CJCOHN's tireless volunteer, Linda Gilbert, for the great work they continue to do.

What's going on in your community? I'll bet you can find several opportunities to make a difference.

Loving thoughts and prayers continue for the communities of Benton and Paron, who lost a much-loved minister. The legacy of Calvin Turbyfill will live on in the hearts of so many young people. We all learned so much from him. For one thing, the proper response to someone who tries to talk us into something we know we shouldn't do: "No thanks, I'm trying to do better." We also learned not to put too much emphasis on the worries of the world. We can all quote one of his favorite verses, Matthew 6:33 (NKJV): "But seek first the kingdom of God and His righteousness and all these things will be added." The most fitting tribute we can offer is to cheerfully continue about our Father's business. Our goal: to see our "brother" Calvin again when our work is through.

Know Your Limits —
Then Give 'Em a Nudge

When we were young, the words "I can't do that" were rarely uttered. We wanted to try it all, and were pretty sure there was nothing beyond our capabilities. There was also no reason to say no to adding more and more to our schedule. We had limitless energy, and thought there was no reason we couldn't fill every hour of every day with fun activities.

In junior high school, I was a little taller and a little heavier than most of the other girls. Since my physical education teacher was quite a bit shorter, she didn't feel comfortable "spotting" me when we were learning gymnastic moves. So, while the smaller girls were doing handsprings and cartwheels, I was mastering somersaults and other things that kept me closer to the ground.

I also remember not being the fastest one in gym class. When we did laps around the small lake across from the school, I was satisfied with completing the race, and didn't worry about having the fastest time.

The closest I ever came to being an athlete was when I was a member of the marching band in high school. This appealed to me first because of my love for music, but the marching thing turned out to be fun, and provided a way to stay in shape in the bargain. This is also when my sister and my mother and I learned about time management. Mom was adamant that we participate in as many school activities as we wanted, so we were not allowed to have jobs that would interfere in any way. I picked up a little extra cash babysitting, but enjoyed being a member of the band, the choir, and the drama club, as well as church activities and Girl Scouts. If there were limits imposed, we never felt them.

After hubby and I started a family of our own, things seemed to change. First, we pushed our own interests to the back burner, as the kids took up all of our time. We both had to work long hours just to keep them in food and diapers, and then when they got in school, to allow them to participate in their own activities. With three offspring, choices were made, and limits on the number of things they could be involved in were a difficult reality.

Eventually, all three chose the same two things that had been most important to us as children: Scouts and band. This kept the whole family plenty busy, and soon every night of the week was packed with one activity or another. We learned several quick and easy recipes for suppers on the go, and go we did, in the typical all-American minivan. We were on the sidelines, hauling equipment, chaperoning band trips, serving refreshments tailgate style.

We eventually became the folks who stood in front of the school cafeteria to try to convince parents to become leaders. The script we were reading from said, "Isn't your child worth just one hour a week?" I didn't read that part, because in truth it took a lot more time than that. But the sentiment was the same. They were worth it. Their childhood would be short, and in the blink of an eye, they would be gone, with families of their own to support.

Limits really boil down to priorities. For those who choose to be athletes, staying in condition and practicing becomes more important than anything else. Adults who want to spend time with their children find the time by sacrificing other things.

The older we get, the more our bodies play into the scheme of things. If we didn't make exercise a priority when we were younger, it becomes harder now. So, when our time is freed up as our children require less of our attention, our bodies won't allow us to try those long-suspended activities. Limits become very real.

There is a fine line, though, between recognizing limits and giving up. It would be easy to dismiss an idea with, "Sorry, I haven't been able to do that in years." Or, "I just don't have the time for that." Oh yes, sitting in that recliner in front of some meaningless display on a flickering screen is relaxing and appealing. The more we do it, the easier it is to continue.

I know that my body needs more rest now. But, I know that even though it may be tougher than it used to be, I need to continue to get up and move. And maybe I won't be the voice at the front of the room, or the one riding the school bus to the next competition, but surely there is time to be a part, to stay involved. All I need is an occasional nudge.

You Might Be a Hog Fan

A popular comedian has a routine in which he shares tell-tale signs that you may be a redneck. In the midst of another football season, you can tell you are a real fan if you have a list like what follows—my ten most memorable Razorback games. These are in chronological order, because there is no way I could rank the memories from best to worst. They are all a part of the fabric that makes up the lives of the people I love the most.

1. *Arkansas vs. Texas A & M, War Memorial Stadium in Little Rock, 1975*: My former boyfriend gave me and my new fiancé tickets to a game in December that was televised. While generous ex watched from the comfort of his couch, future hubby and I almost literally froze in the end zone. I remember driving his precious Dodge Challenger through the bumper to bumper traffic. I was very surprised while researching for this column to learn that we actually won that game. The score did not play into my memories at all. I was happy to be with a great guy, but longing for a warmer location!

2. *Arkansas vs. Tulsa, Fayetteville, 1976:* As newlyweds, we drove up to the Ozarks with some friends and witnessed a defensive duel, highlighted by two record-setting field goal kickers: Steve Cox of Tulsa and Steve Little of Arkansas. Tulsa kicked three of them, and the Hogs only managed one. The final score 9-3 Tulsa.

3. *Arkansas vs. LSU, Little Rock, 1996:* Our oldest son,

75

with money from his first job burning a hole in his pocket, bought tickets for himself and his dad. A friend who was a State Legislator at the time let us use his passes, so the whole family went on a cold, rainy weekend after Thanksgiving and stayed for most of a miserable defeat. I remember that the purple and gold ponchos outnumbered the red ones by quite a bit when we finally made our way to the exits.

4. *Parents' Day in Fayetteville, Arkansas vs. Alabama, 1998:* While recalling that game today, my son's comment was, "Were y'all at that game?" We watched the action from the student section, and observed our college freshman having the time of his life in the end zone. A big 42-6 win that cemented our fervor for all things cardinal and white.

5. *Arkansas-28, Tennessee-24, Fayetteville, 1999:* We watched on television as our college student spent the weekend after his 21st birthday helping his friends dismantle the goal posts after a glorious game. He still owns a baggie with a piece of the turf from that game. Some relics are more precious than gold.

6. *Arkansas vs. Tennessee, September 2001:* Just days before the world changed forever, we were seated on metal seats at the very tip-top of the newly remodeled stadium during severe thunderstorm warnings. After several back and forth trips to the safety of the concourse, hubby and I decided we would be better off watching on the television in our hotel room. Our kids wanted to divorce us that day, but we've gotten over it…well most of us have.

Anyway, Tennessee won.

7. *Seven Overtimes, Arkansas vs. Mississippi in Oxford, 2001:*
    I actually watched this from a hospital bed after knee
    surgery. My future son-in-law was keeping an eye on
    the heart monitor and threatened to turn the
    television off if I didn't calm down. Calm? Not a
    chance. Arkansas-58, Mississippi-56.

8. *War Memorial Stadium, Arkansas vs. Louisiana, Monroe,
    2004:* Our second son had graduated from the U of
    A by this time, and he came to town for the game.
    We bought tickets from a scalper outside the
    stadium, and had terrific seats next to the Razorback
    band in the end zone. Son was still in full-on student
    mode, and performed all of the songs right along
    with them. We won the game, but it wouldn't have
    mattered to us in the least.

9. *Arkansas vs. Mississippi State at Starkville, MS, 2008:*
    This was a road trip with our son's fiancée and his
    friends from Memphis. Our now daughter-in-law
    still remembers that my husband made her leave
    her warmest coat in the car because it was the
    wrong color. We left when the game seemed lost,
    only to hear a rally as we were leaving. Our son
    pulled in and out of the parking space to get the
    best reception on the radio. Final score: Mississippi
    State-31, Arkansas-28.

10. *Arkansas vs. Auburn, Fayetteville, 2009:* After a
    terribly difficult week that included the funeral of
    someone we all loved, we took a very refreshing trip
    to the top of The Hill. A great victory, 44-23. How
    'bout them Hawgs, indeed.

A bonus memory that doesn't directly include me: After my oldest son married, his wife and I stayed at their apartment in Fayetteville while "the boys" went to the Auburn game. They had two student tickets and a spouse ticket between them, and only one of them was an actual student. Dad was told to try to act like a professor, and brother was praying no one would challenge his "spouse" status.

The Razorbacks are more than our favorite team; they are part of our lives. Here's hoping your family has some memories together that will last long after the final seconds click off the stadium clock. Woo Pig Sooie!!

Resurgence of Hope

Note to Michelle Obama: I understand what you meant about your renewed feeling of patriotism, even if your choice of words was unfortunate. I feel it too.

Note to my Republican-leaning friends: Please don't stop reading yet. The intent of this column is certainly not to persuade anyone on how to vote in any election. Instead, I'm just recognizing and hoping to encourage something positive that seems to be happening in our country.

Young people are excited about politics again.

The 40th anniversary of the assassination of Robert Kennedy reminded me of a childhood hurt that has never quite healed. I vividly remember watching the funeral of President John Kennedy. I recall his tiny son saluting as the casket passed, and his daughter, about my age, trying to act grown up and brave. I couldn't imagine why anyone would want to kill someone so strong and good.

By 1968, at age 10, I was aware that there were people who resisted change at any cost. They seemed to fear that granting rights to other people would diminish their own chances at the American dream. So, I was extremely sad, but not shocked, when Martin Luther King, Jr. was killed. During that awful time, a new voice emerged to comfort us. The president's brother, Bobby, made America feel like things could somehow be right again.

Then, one terrible morning in June, the radio in my bedroom replayed the chaotic events of the previous night in a hotel in California. I listened in disbelief as I started putting together the dreadful bottom line. Another of my heroes was dead. Though the three killers did not seem to be connected at all, I sensed a conspiracy. It seemed that everyone who worked toward unifying the country was doomed.

A popular folk song, "Abraham, Martin and John", pulled at our heartstrings: "Anybody here seen my old friend Bobby? Can you tell me where he's gone? He freed a lot of people, but it seems the good die young. I just looked around, and he's gone."

Though many people of my generation remained interested in politics, we developed a defeatist attitude. Perhaps nothing we did made a difference. We got another glimmer of hope when the Clintons went to Washington. Here in the Ouachita area, we were filled with hometown pride. Gradually, the face of America began to change, to become a little more tolerant and respectful.

Fast forward to 2008. Where are we now? Many of the awful memories of discrimination are incomprehensible to our children and grandchildren. Hateful things still happen, but they are not accepted or overlooked. Cold cases from years ago are finally being prosecuted. Careers are often ruined over jokes or crude remarks that are heard when microphones are supposed to be turned off. And for the first time, we have a presidential candidate with an African American background. The waves of change are sweeping the country.

During the recent primaries, the faces of the candidates' supporters looked a little different, too. A large percentage were young, and very enthusiastic. The internet helped to reach the masses with the idea that America could rebound from the down period we are currently in. Hopefully, regardless of the outcome of the election, this new feeling will continue. Our country is worth getting excited about, Conservative or Liberal, whatever your racial or religious background.

America, here's another chance. Don't blow it this time.

Be Thankful in ALL Things

This time of year, we spend a lot of time expressing our happiness about the blessings we have been given in life. Our homes, our jobs, our perfectly beautiful kids and grandkids. When we start listing good things, our cup runneth over.

But what about the times when circumstances are less than perfect? When life seems to be giving us more lemons than anyone needs to make a good batch of lemonade? Can we really be thankful in those difficult times as well?

I spent thirty-five years working for the State of Arkansas. Though not always paid as well as comparable employees in the private sector, I did have an attractive retirement plan, so I began marking off my calendar when I was in my forties, planning for that magical date when I could stay at home and start drawing a retirement check.

My husband worked very hard as well, in a job that he was extremely good at, but that was hard on him physically. Suddenly, our whole world was rocked when the sagging housing industry caused his long-time employers to lay him off. Though quite a shock to both our systems, things eventually worked out quite well. He now has another job that he loves, and that is not as damaging to his health. I retired for a short time, and then returned to work in a less stressful position that allows a little more time to concentrate on my writing. Looking back, we are both thankful for that particular economic downturn.

As an avowed aficionado of social media, I am following a family with a much more dramatic story. This young couple received devastating news very early in their first pregnancy. Advised by physicians that their unborn child was severely handicapped, and would most likely not survive to be born alive, terminating the pregnancy seemed to be the best option. Because of their belief that God has a better plan, they decided to continue, and prepared to love this child for as long as they were allowed.

The mother of the baby started posting the day their daughter was born. She survived, to the surprise of all of the medical experts. You can get the medical details on their Facebook page entitled "Prayers for the Pragels", but the bottom line is that eight months later, this little miracle brings all of us the most amazing smiles anyone can imagine. With an underdeveloped brain, each milestone in her life is totally unexpected, and cause for immediate rejoicing.

It might be hard for the immediate family to be thankful for this sweetheart's diagnosis, but I know that the medical world must be. They are learning so much from her, and she is so inspiring to others who are going through similar issues. We are all thankful that her brave parents are sharing their journey.

We frequently worship with a congregation of Christians that has continued to thrive beyond all expectations. Their beginnings came about because of a disagreement between their minister and the congregation he was serving. Feeling that he had no choice, he and a few close friends decided to worship together in any space that was available. That first place turned out to be the city hall of a small town in our region. Borrowing song books, chairs, and communion supplies, they pressed on and actually thrived.

Their next meeting place was in an old service

station/convenience store. This "cozy" space was often filled to capacity, and the excitement with which they approached their weekly services was palpable. As we speak, the congregation of around 70, and sometimes many more, has moved to a new building, built for the most part through the love and labor of the members. No one would have ever expected to be thankful for a painful division with other believers, but one day, when the origins of this group are discussed, that may not be such a strange idea.

Once, a little girl in Southeast Kansas was devastated when her parents divorced. The next few years were a struggle on many fronts, but eventually her mother met and married a man from Arkansas. They moved to Saline County just before the girl's senior year in high school, and the rest, as they say, is history. If I could speak to that little girl today, would I tell her that one day she would be thankful for the intense pain she felt? Of course not. But with the benefit of many years of hindsight, I would have to admit that even that experience was one that I would never trade.

Let us be Thankful.

A Season for Reflection

As the busy autumn activities continue, we begin to plan for the grand finale of the year: the holiday season. Of course, retail outlets are starting their big push earlier and earlier, but for most of us, Halloween signals that fall is almost gone, and it's time to start planning our Thanksgiving menu. My own thoughts become more sentimental as I look around and miss the faces that will not be around my table. I try to emphasize counting my blessings, instead of preparing for a two-month pity party. Looking back at the joys of the past, appreciating every moment of the present, I get ready for the greatest celebration—the one that commemorates the birth of our Savior. It all leads up to Christmas.

Forty Years: Gone in a Blink

So, I am sure you have heard that the time machine DeLorean from the *Back to the Future* movies has arrived in our current time, which is, as far as I can tell, its final destination. So, if no one has a need for it today, do you think I could borrow it?

Our first stop: an autumn day in 1975. While James Carlisle is working at Congo Mercantile, we swiftly remove the time machine mechanism from the car that Michael J. Fox made famous, and install it in James's 1971 Dodge Challenger. (You ask how we do that? Don't bother me with details.) Okay. Now, we make our one and only change to history during this adventure. James takes a different route to pick me up for our date that night, thereby avoiding the awful crash that ended the Challenger's useful life. (James thankfully emerged relatively unscathed, by the way.)

So, now with the correct car in the picture, our journey continues. Next stop, May 31, 1976. Faith Lutheran Church, Little Rock, Arkansas, where a wedding is taking place. Looking around, we see lots of happy folks, dressed in their Sunday best, even though it is actually Monday (Memorial Day) evening. The young ladies seem to be sporting the same hairstyle: long, straight and shiny, with the young men almost the same, except maybe just a little shorter. The bridesmaids are wearing a light blue calico print dress that will hang in the closet from this day forward. Each is also sporting a wide picture hat. The boys (sorry, men), including the groom, are wearing identical light blue polyester tuxedos with white shirts and light blue bow ties. Jenny's dress, made from the same pattern as the bridesmaids, is a simply beautiful concoction of white satin and lace, with no train, and a simple veil, in the "end of the hippy era" peasant style.

Happy smiles are the order of the day, and history is made as both of Jenny's grandmothers spend time in the same room while remaining civil to each other. Also, the groom is meeting the bride's father for the very first time, and his tough state policeman demeanor does not scare her intended away.

We leave this happy group and speed quickly to another location in Little Rock: the tuxedo shop in downtown Little Rock where our 1976 group was outfitted. The year on the calendar behind the counter displays 2002. Today, James and Jenny are arranging to order a tuxedo for another groom, their oldest son, Chris. They will also order the outfit of the day for Chris's younger brother, Jon, who, along with James, will be one of the groomsmen. They ask for suggestions on a suit for Chris and Jon's young nephew, Jordan, who at 2 months will be too small for the clothing they have on display. It is decided that the baby's mother, Chris and Jon's younger sister, Carrie, who is also in the wedding party, will have to shop elsewhere for the appropriate suit and tie.

Jenny happens to mention the old pale blue masterpieces from years ago, and the clerk says. "Oh yes, we still have those in the attic." A mischievous gleam enters James's eye as he asks, "I don't suppose you would let me borrow one of those jackets for the wedding rehearsal?" In view of the amount of the check we are writing that day, this request is quickly accommodated. Chris's sweet bride, Katherine, was about to learn just what she was getting into by joining this family.

More happy smiles, one more bouquet tossed at a Little Rock church. This time, the guests blow bubbles instead of throwing rice. The bride and groom head off to their honeymoon in Las Vegas, while Jon and Carrie lament items lost when Jon's car is burglarized in the church parking lot during the rehearsal dinner.

Back in the time machine Challenger, James and I speed through the next 14 years, arriving at Northside Church of Christ in Benton, just in time for a Sunday afternoon 40th anniversary reception.

This time, friends and family gather at a party coordinated by the three kids and their spouses. Not an easy task, as they live in Arkansas, Florida, and Texas. All five grandchildren will be in attendance. As is usually the case, the chatter of the cousins will be dominated by plans for "Granny Camp", when all of them spend time with their grandparents. Spoiler alert: this year's event has been renamed to "Grand-cation", and it promises to be a once in a lifetime trip for all involved.

After an appropriate amount of cake and punch is consumed and happy memories are shared, we leave in the time machine Challenger again. This will be the most difficult part of the plan to pull off. I take the wheel and drive to the nearby car lot that now sells vehicles that look much like this seventies' classic. We park it among its shinier counterparts, and try to imagine the look on the salesman's face when he discovers it. The time machine can be utilized as needed by the lucky new owners. I take James's hand as we walk off into the I-30 sunset together. Because, truth be told, there is no need to change a minute of our past. And the future is bright ahead.

The Best Gifts

An early memory of my grandmother was the task she would assign us after Thanksgiving dinner. She would sit us down with a paper and pencil and ask us for a list of presents we wanted for Christmas. The first time, I let my imagination wander, and listed several things that attracted my attention while browsing the Sears and Roebuck catalog. On Christmas morning, I was embarrassed to find that every single thing I had listed was under the tree for me, from Granny. Santa Claus was left with very little to bring. Many of the items had been just fleeting ideas, and while pulling off the ribbons and paper, I couldn't recall asking for that particular toy or game.

The next year, with a little more wisdom under my belt, I gave the list some thought, and only wrote down one thing. Granny provided prompts. "Maybe a nice dress?" she suggested. "Or, what about music? Write down some of your favorite songs."

In my robe and slippers that December 25th, I was glad to receive the special item I had wanted (though I certainly can't remember what it was all these years later). The dress came from the finest department store in Granny's city, and for each song I requested, she purchased the whole album, instead of the single I was expecting. One of the most popular songs of the day was a novelty piece called "Rubber Duckie." True to form, I received the whole album of *Sesame Street* favorites. Since I was in 7th grade that year, I am quite sure I was the only one of my friends who received that particular gift.

I began to dread finishing my pumpkin pie. I wished that

Granny would take my list as a suggestion, not a purchase order. I hated appearing ungrateful, but I also didn't like having the rest of the family think I was asking for too much. So, I followed the lead of my older cousins, and asked Granny for cash so that I could do my own shopping. I felt a little regret. I think she really enjoyed the hunt, the quest to bring us exactly the items we had asked for, in the perfect color and size. But, come Christmas morning, I was truly grateful, and didn't have to endure the scrutiny of the rest of the family as I opened present after present.

Flash forward past years of struggling to provide our own children with at least one of the very special items they dreamed of. Santa always managed to come through somehow.

At a time of my life when we are able to purchase most of what we need and want throughout the year, there are not a lot of things on my Christmas list these days. My husband does know me very well, however. So, he enjoys picking out one particular gift that will always make me smile, an addition to the Christmas village that graces my entryway. This indulges my love of decorating, and also sparks my imagination. One day, a holiday book is bound to be set in my very own itty-bitty town.

My favorite gifts are much less expensive, but infinitely more satisfying. I was presented with some of them over the past holiday weekend. A six-year-old grandson took comfort in my lap after a long day of family celebration. A precious granddaughter wanted to be involved with meal preparation, and loved to brag about the special cake she and her mom made for us. My increasingly sullen teenaged grand presented me with joyful laughter as he and I played a rousing game of air hockey. The nine-year-old and his smaller cousin shared some heartfelt hugs as they headed for home.

I am looking forward to a few more of these fabulous presents when we travel to see the newest member of the family. I can't wait for those bright-eyed giggles and sloppy kisses.

I can't help thinking that the happiness I feel at this time of year must be much like the emotions that surrounded that manger in Bethlehem so long ago. After centuries of stories were passed from one generation to another, God was fulfilling His promise to send a king. No one could predict exactly what would take place in the life of that little baby. But there was wild, unbridled joy in the air. So much amazement at the unbelievable gift they had been given. So much hope for the future. Joy to the world! Oh, come let us adore Him!

May you receive all of His best gifts this holiday season, and look forward to a bright and beautiful new year.

Christmas Collections

If we had our druthers, there would be two Christmas trees at our house each year. My husband's would be elegantly appointed with beautiful, trendy decorations, probably all in the same color family. His might completely change from year to year. Mine, on the other hand, would display the same treasures I carefully store away at each year's end. As I write this, they are still boxed up, but when you read it, they'll be in a place of honor in the corner of our living room.

After thirty-five years of collecting, I have more ornaments than I can practically place on the tall but skinny imitation pine with plastic holly berries and fake twists of grapevine worked in. So, as I decorate, I'll just pull some of the precious pieces out and pause for a moment as I place them back into their home for protection.

There are ornaments fashioned by my children when they were small. Created from ideas in craft books owned by a clever teacher, they may have started as a clothespin, or a jar lid. Paint, ribbon, glue, and glitter transformed them into something wonderful, a tiny piece of a child's heart. As they say in the credit card commercial: Priceless.

Then, there are the dated ornaments purchased over the years, one for each year of our married life. The designs reflect the times and the budget constraints of those years. Some celebrate a big event in our family, like "Baby's First Christmas." Others were purchased at after-Christmas sales. Each brings along a flood of been-there-done-that memories.

My mother has long upheld a tradition of making

ornaments for our family's trees. Hers show imagination and creativity, and always bring to mind the reasons for the season, love and family. I followed her lead for several years, so you'll find some examples of my feeble attempts at craftiness. Teddy bears with ribbons and bells, scraps of leather with cut-outs from old Christmas cards, rings made from a special, inedible dough.

Not all of the ornaments are homemade or inexpensive. Otherwise, they'd all be relegated to the back of the tree by my "curb-appeal"-conscious hubby. We do own some really nice ones, including part of a Norman Rockwell collection purchased by my stepmother sometime during the last century. There are also tributes to our favorite sports teams, and a few with Disney connections.

I must confess that my Christmas collecting isn't confined to the tree. You'll find memorable items displayed on almost every flat surface in the house. One, in an honored position on top of the dining room hutch, even belongs to my husband. Yes, he looks forward each year to seeing the Santa Claus doll (well, that's what it is) his parents purchased for him on a Christmas shopping trip to Benton when he was small. It really is all about the happy memories this time of year.

One of my favorite Christmas stories brings home the fact that God is a collector, too. The difference is that, He desires to collect our souls for protection from the evils of this world, and to provide a permanent home with Him.

The story goes something like this: There was a man who was raised as a Christian, but had become cynical after years of existing in our rather self-absorbed world. While his wife and kids went to a Christmas Eve program at church, he stayed home and watched out the window as a strong winter storm brewed. The wind howled, the cold blizzard raged, and he saw a large flock of birds battling the wind, looking for some form of refuge. He'd often enjoyed feeding and watching birds, and his heart was touched by their struggle. He glanced at the large barn that stood behind their house, and he was inspired. Bundling up, he hurried out to the building, threw open the door, and turned on the lights, hoping to lure the floundering creatures to safety. The flock continued to fly hither and yon, and none made their way into the warmth and protection of the barn. The man finally gave up and returned inside, leaving the door and lights as an open invitation.

When his family returned home, he told them of his efforts, and a strange realization touched him as he spoke these words: "If only I could have turned myself into a bird; then I could have guided them in…"

This Christmas, as you collect happy memories, remember the perfect plan of your heavenly Father. He still wants to draw you closer. Let the baby in the manger be your guide.

Thinking Outside the Christmas Box

We all get them: Christmas cards with nostalgic Currier and Ives scenes of a snow-covered countryside and carolers bundled in fur. Pretty to look at, but for most of us, nothing like our own holiday memories.

Our unique backgrounds make our recollections as individual as we are. At this time of year, they're fun to look back on, even if no one else recognizes them as traditional. Two things that always remind me of Christmas: diesel fumes and automatic milking machines.

Don't get me wrong, there are a few things rattling around in my memory banks that would fit into a Capra movie. The toy and hobby store in our little hometown did have an electric train set up for display during December. We loved to watch it make its way around the miniature village, across the trestles and through the tunnels. We knew there was no way it would look like that in our living room.

In our town, Santa Claus set up his headquarters in a tiny house in the community park. My sister and I waited in the frigid, twisting line to be sure he knew exactly what our requests for the year involved. One year, when we had decided that St. Nick must have lots of helpers to cover his large territory, the jolly fellow called us each by name. Could it be that he was the Real One? I'm still not sure about that.

So, you're wondering about the diesel fumes? Easy. When I was about eight, which would make my sister six or so, we made a bus trip to see Granny. Mom introduced us to the driver, and he posted us in the seat directly behind him. At each stop, he'd either accompany us inside for a quick break, or instruct us to stay put as we loaded and unloaded more travelers. I felt extremely grown up in the position of being "in charge" of my younger sibling. At the end of the less than 200-mile journey, we were claimed by our grandmother in an indoor terminal—full of diesel fumes. That smell still takes me back.

Of course, over the years there were lots of Christmas trees. Many were hauled across town on the top of Mom's Volkswagen Bug. We must have made quite a scene, and surely lifted a few spirits, as we passed our neighbors' windows. Once home, it took all sorts of manipulations and contraptions to keep the tree upright for the days remaining until package-opening time. This was complicated by the decorating style my sister and I employed: most everything on one side of the lower branches.

The milking machines? Logical. When Christmas was hosted at our house, my mom had to come up with activities for the cousins. Granny's preparations for Santa's visit went much better without so many little ones under foot. There were not many tourist attractions near our Southeast Kansas home, and even fewer open on Christmas Eve afternoon. The solution? A very busy dairy on the far side of town that had a big window across the side of their milking barn. The friendly ladies who starred in this show were as reliable as clockwork. At the appointed times each day, passersby could watch as workers took care of the "hooking up" process that produced our favorite beverage. After squirming around in the cold to watch from start to squirty finish, we loaded back into the car and sang Christmas carols all the way back.

Of course, the centerpiece of every celebration was, and still is, the birth day of the most important Man in all of our lives. One of my most memorable gifts was a Bible from Santa Claus. It was good to know that even he knew the real reason for the season. Still displayed proudly in my mom's house is a nativity scene that has been lovingly placed since my granny was small. Its pieces worn, and even broken, from too much attention from small hands, it is the perfect reminder of the most precious gift any of us has ever been given.

May your Christmas be filled with His peace, as you make your own memories. No matter how quirky, they'll always be yours.

Christmas: The Ultimate Comfort Zone

Before you really get started reading this column, close your eyes for just a minute, and picture yourself on Christmas morning. Really. I promise I'll be here when you get back. One, two, three, close 'em.

Open again? Okay. So, where were you? What were you doing? What did you see, hear, smell?

I'll share first. I am at my grandmother's house. The house is quiet, except for Granny's humming as she cooks. I can hear the clicking of her basset hound's toenails on the linoleum floor as she follows Granny around the kitchen. The smell of corned beef hash wafts through the living room. The little aluminum Christmas tree glows brightly in the reflected light of the round multi-colored light machine. Unwrapped toys still sit under the tree, with neatly folded bathrobes and slippers and other warm clothes nearby. We would have a quiet breakfast, just my mom and sister and me and Granny (and Sam the Basset hound). Soon, my aunt and cousins will return for dinner and playing outside in the South Central Kansas snow.

Your memories are probably much different. But it is not hard to conjure up a Christmas memory. They stick and stay in our heads, and we bring them out when we need to be in a happy place.

If I try again, and fast forward to when our kids were small, the scene will be similar. Some presents are unwrapped under an artificially green tree in our living room, but Santa's special surprises: a Cabbage Patch doll, a Pound Puppy, and a new pair of cowboy boots wait proudly for the first sleepyhead to emerge from the bedroom. I sit with my cup of hot tea and soak up the precious silence. Santa had come through once again, though my husband and I had wondered how he would manage with our meager paychecks. Outside, the Arkansas sun shines brightly, and I am actually thankful that there is no snow. Here in the foothills of the Ouachitas, slick roads would keep the grandparents from coming over later to watch the kids enjoy their new things. The big dinner the night before was at their house, and I will most likely serve sandwiches today, along with any leftovers that might arrive with them. For now, heavenly peace.

Yes, the faces around the tree change, the size and value of the presents vary, but there are constants. Things seem familiar, comfortable.

Now that our kids are grown, our new normal is that we very rarely manage to have all of our offspring in the same room at the same time. We enjoy each one when we get to see them, no matter the date on the calendar. The tree goes up earlier and stays up longer to accommodate their schedules. That is fine for me, as I have more of those quiet moments, more time to remember Christmases past.

Not everyone adjusts to changes in the Christmas routine as easily. The same memories that bring us joy also cause pain. The absence of familiar faces diminishes our joy. We need to be aware of this, and reach out to those who suffer during the holidays.

The first Christmas was not comfortable for the young couple who had traveled a great distance to find a "No Vacancy" sign, and a baby who was born in a building intended for animals. They knew, though, that something amazing was happening, having heard from angels, and visitors who came to gaze in amazement at the future king. This story is the constant that keeps Christmas so special for all of us. The realization that no matter what else happens in this world, God keeps His promises. Whether in a festive room full of friends and family, or alone in the flickering light of a fireplace, Christmas encourages us, prompts us to look around, to reach out to each other. Let's remember the hope that filled that tiny, smelly stable so long ago. Comfortable or not, enjoy your Christmas celebration this year!

What's Really Important

Over recent years, I have watched enough television on non-network channels to diagnose my own condition. I am quite certain I am not a hoarder. I don't keep candy bar wrappers or stack up egg cartons. I am not a collector, either. If I buy a stuffed toy or popular movie, it certainly does not stay in its original package, and I'm not obsessed about having every piece from any set.

No, what I am is a "treasurer." Make no mistake; I am not volunteering to be the club member in charge of collecting dues and paying bills. What I mean is that I do tend to keep a few objects around longer than other non-afflicted people might count as normal, but it is all because of the connection, the stories that go along with these items. One man's junk becomes my treasure.

I am certain to be able to provide a story for every unusual item you might find in my house. The brass bells hanging on the door between my kitchen and my laundry room set up a happy cacophony every time someone moves that door. They made the same noise in my grandmother's house when I was a child. I was certain that I would have to fight to remove them from her estate, but evidently those memories were not as vivid for my cousins, so in this granny's house is where they now reside.

In the corner of our dining room, a handsome corner hutch holds plates, cups, knick knacks. It is the hutch itself that is important, as it was crafted by my very talented husband, in our own garage. Go ahead, try and name a price for that. Your efforts will be fruitless.

Another handcrafted item sits in my bedroom, holding a potted plant. This little three-legged table was made by my father when he was a student in a high school shop class. For years, it held the rotary-dial telephone in the heart of our house. Since the cord didn't reach very far, I held many a whispered conversation in its vicinity during my early teens.

Hanging on the living room wall is a more modern decoration. A little ballet of clock movements is performed at the top of each hour. Purchased by my mother at a local jewelry store, she said it was advanced payment for the trouble she was bound to cause me in her later years. These days, it brings a constant melodious smile to my world.

Of course, there are also more traditional keepsakes. Photo albums, scrapbooks, and journals all give a very tangible picture of the members of my family past and present. For me, the handwritten thoughts are as precious as the visual reminders. I have a tiny glimpse of who that person was on the inside.

I was reminded of these things when a young family member recently lost her home and many of her possessions in a fire. The community will help provide the necessities of daily living, furniture, clothing, dishes, appliances. But what of those special little items that hold so much significance? Those losses leave a person really feeling empty, I am sure.

In Steve Martin's movie, *The Jerk*, he is being evicted from his house, and is selecting a few items to take along with him. Loosely quoted, "All I need," the character says, "is this chair. And my teddy bear, and this drinking glass." As he wanders through the house, each item he passes reaches out, and he can't bear to leave any of it. He soon becomes overburdened with important stuff. It's not the monetary value, it's the emotional attachment that we feel along with him.

At this point in our lives, hubby and I are trying to downsize, and the possibility exists that we might soon have to pack up our important stuff to take to a new location. Decisions will be made, items will be looked at with fresh eyes. Is it really important that I keep the toys my kids played with as children? Probably not. But that little dime-store statue of a pair of swans one of them bought with his own allowance as a Mother's Day gift? The silver jewelry box engraved with "Mom" purchased when my oldest son and his fiancée were shopping for gifts for their wedding attendants? The Precious Moments figurine that sat on my daughter's dresser until she left to start her own household?

In the words of the little Chihuahua in the old commercial: "I think I need a bigger box."

A Season for
Relaunching

The only thing constant in this life is change. That is not my original thought, of course, but it holds so much truth. The things that seem the most reliable, the people we love and look to for help and reassurance, all pass away. These changes frighten us, but somehow, at the same time give us hope. We realize we are a part of something much bigger. We know that God has the whole thing figured out. Each transition just allows for other wonderful things to happen, for people who have grown stronger to step forward and take their rightful place. We look back at the lives our loved ones have lived, and look forward to what our own lives will become because of them.

A Matter of Trust

Eastern Kansas during the Depression years was not an easy place to raise a family. My grandparents moved back and forth from my grandfather's home territory to my grandmother's. This was probably partially for job purposes, but my grandfather didn't always make the move along with the rest of them. A very hard thing, especially for little Donnie, the youngest of the "first three." He told me that the worst year of his schooling was the second grade (or was it third?) when he changed schools, losing all his friends, and having to struggle to "start over" in his subjects. My mother said he told her about leaving his old home and watching his favorite Irish setter running to try to keep up with the car as they were leaving it behind.

This early turmoil made it very hard for my dad to form attachments of any kind, as there always seemed to be a fear of losing the pets, places, and even people you loved.

He and my mom met in Mulvane, Kansas, which had been the home of his mother. This was a thriving, very happy little town in the 1940s. Here, the younger two siblings were born, but their father continued to be an in-and-out presence in the family.

My daddy was not a big story teller, but mostly from my mom, and from my dad's younger brother and sister, I have heard some wonderful tales of their upbringing. There is even a story of a nosy telephone operator straight out of the *Andy Griffith* show, who would advise my aunt to head for home, instead of connecting her to my grandmother when she wanted to stay a little longer at a friend's house.

Another tale relates my dad's first job, and his first experience with driving. Having never tried to drive, at somewhere under legal driving age, he was hired by the local dairy to drive the milk delivery truck. So, he did, causing quite a panic when he showed up at home in the huge vehicle.

Merry Lu and Donnie became an item when she was a senior in high school. She and her family had arrived from California, living first on a farm at the edge of town, and then in a house just a few blocks from the McLeod kids. Pictures from that time show a fun-loving couple in blue jeans, white shirts, and Oxford shoes. Mom's sister Donna married one of my dad's best friends, who was also raised right there in Mulvane. My dad's dad even baked my parents' wedding cake, in my mom's mom's kitchen!

Daddy's love of adventure fit right in with another job, at the local Boeing plant. Here, he photographed the historic planes that were being used in the Korean conflict, and quite logically, enlisted in the Air Force. I never heard him say if he wanted to be a pilot, but I know he was fascinated by airplanes, so being around them in any way possible was a perfect fit.

In the military, he discovered his love for law enforcement, and after his enlistment ended, he came home to enter the Kansas Highway Patrol. This was truly his niche. He was well respected and popular in the communities he served, even showing up in a feature article in the *Kansas City Star* when he worked on the Kansas Turnpike.

Friends and family knew him for his dry sense of humor and his bellowing laugh. He loved to tease, but in a gentle way. It was really more like "poking fun" and was well received. His nieces and nephews dubbed him "Unca Donald" because of his very accurate imitation of Donald Duck.

Of course, from my perspective, he was a wonderful daddy. Large enough to have a great big lap for cuddling, but fit and agile enough to love playing with us. Fond of driving, so always ready for an adventure, or a trip to the lake for a swim or a picnic.

I think the most memorable trait, though was trust-worthiness. This may seem ironic, since he and my mom divorced when I was five years old. But, he never made a promise to me that he didn't keep. Before I learned to swim, I remember him carrying me in the water that was clearly over my head. I asked him not to let my head go under the water, and I knew I could trust him to be sure that didn't happen until I was ready.

Looking back, I think I owe my love for reading and writing stories to him. We had spent hours on the front porch swing reading before I started school. Then, after he moved away, our back-and-forth letters helped me develop a "voice" as I related the everyday excitement of elementary school. Once, I put the wrong piece of paper in the envelope, and he sent it back. "Well, it looks like you deserve a pretty good grade on this spelling paper. What did the teacher think of the letter you meant to send to me?"

Sister and I went to visit him once a year for a week, and he would show up exactly on time to the minute. When I was grown, he didn't make promises for exactly this reason. Once, he was supposed to come to Arkansas for a visit, and a tornado lifted his house off the foundations. He was so apologetic when he called to say it would not be a good time for that visit.

When he met the love of his life, my sister and I were still very young. I recall that we had visited Ann when they were dating, as she lived just a few blocks away from his house. But then there was a special picnic (I remember we took a pizza to the park) when he told us that they intended to be married. Even though I was little, I remembered feeling honored that he wanted our "permission" before they went ahead with their plans.

With Ann's help, he even allowed himself to become attached to pets. I remember that she had a chihuahua before they married, and then they had teacup poodles, always a pair at a time. It was a joy to see this teddy bear of a man cuddling a tiny ball of fluff.

When his beloved Ann became sick, and then passed away, Daddy seemed to understand that time was getting away. He came to Arkansas to visit me, then went to Texas to see my sister, and we crammed the next few years full with calls and visits. When he was too ill to travel, my husband and I made the eight-hour trip to visit him once or twice a month. These brief visits were happy ones, with smiles and encouragement, and even the rare "I love you" spoken aloud.

He was the stereotypical policeman with a gruff manner and a heart of gold. I was so blessed to call him *Daddy*.

Dedicated to Donald Dale McLeod,
October 23, 1931 to August 22, 2003.

The Dad He Didn't Have to Be

By the time Alvie Tuggle came along, my sister and I had adjusted very well to our lives in a single parent home. Our mama did a wonderful job of raising us. Our daddy was right on time with the child support checks, and we enjoyed an annual week-long vacation visiting him and our stepmom. Still, though, my idea of a picture-perfect family had been disrupted when I was five, and I had spent my dreamtime and many of the daylight hours scouting the prospects for a new husband for my mom.

Mom met this handsome man from Arkansas at her job as a bank teller, while cashing his weekly paychecks. He was in town with the construction company that was building our new hospital. When relating the story later, they argued about who was flirting with whom. But, suffice it to say, they were both captivated at first sight. It was quite a treat for two teenaged girls to witness a courtship.

Until that time, I had heard very little about our "catty-corner" neighboring state. We had spent some vacations in Branson, and at Girl Scout camp south of Joplin, but those were in the Missouri quadrant of the Ozarks. Over the next few years, I learned to love the home state of this man who swept all of us off our feet.

He had had a lonely childhood. He told of tumbling down hills with other kids, notably the Cash brothers, Johnny and Tommy, when they visited Little Rock from their home in the northeast part of the state. But no tales of brothers or sisters. The reason for this was the source of much heartache. Alvie's father and mother had each left

123

their first families to be together. This caused much resentment, of course, and unfortunately, Alvie was the innocent victim. So, while he had loving parents, there always seemed to be something hanging over his head.

He learned to work very hard at a young age, hauling rocks and helping his father, who worked as a stone mason. Though he claimed that he hated this heavy, sweaty work, he used his talents in later years, embellishing his home with rock underpinning, a hearth in the family room, and even a fireplace.

His first marriage ended unhappily, and I know he must have hated the fact that he had very little contact with his oldest son in the growing-up years. His second wife already had a daughter, and soon the new couple added another little boy and girl.

My stepsisters and stepbrothers tell many happy stories of weekends spent at the lake, where Alvie loved fishing and water-skiing. These activities, along with this job as a welder and pipe-fitter, kept him happy and fit.

After his second marriage also ended in divorce, he and my mother married, and we moved to Arkansas. Her mission became to unite all the children of all three of these families into one, and she succeeded, with many noisy and happy gatherings in their home and outdoors, where my sister and I were thrown into the mix and learned to love the water and camping as well.

Since he already had experience raising teenaged girls, I think he came into my life at just the right time. He had very strong opinions, and sometimes he was a little off on judging the character of my friends. He and my mom really liked the young man I was dating, because of his impeccable manners and short haircut. This guy's best friend, however was really the sweeter of the two, but because of his long hair, Alvie would have no part of him.

When Mr. Clean-cut treated me badly, though, I didn't hear any defense or excuses as Alvie and I had a heart to heart talk on our front porch swing. He could have easily reacted with the classic line, "boys will be boys." Instead, he said the words I needed to hear. "You deserve much better than that. Someday, you will find the right man who respects you and treats you right." He was correct on both counts, and that young man did come along, after we moved to Arkansas.

I think that maybe my little family came along at just the right time for my stepdad, too. He seemed to really relax, and enjoy life. Of course, there were still difficulties, every family has them. But on the weekends when we were at the lake together, or when the house was full of noisy kids, he actually allowed himself to just be happy.

While he was working, his job sites were often too far away for commuting, and this is when he and my mom really got to test the whole togetherness idea. She quit her job at the bank for a while, and they lived in a travel trailer. By this time, my siblings and I were grown and on our own, so it was just two of them, in that small space, 24/7. Proof that they were made for each other!

After they both retired, they took their little houses on wheels all over the country. Alvie was never one to rest on his laurels, so they hauled a workshop around with all the tools he needed to build woodcrafts. With Mom along to spark his creativity, they built hundreds of decorative items that brought smiles to dozens of craft fairs, and a spark of whimsy and color to front yards all over the world. These happy times just made his blue eyes sparkle even more.

The family gatherings became portable too, and their grandkids have many happy memories of picnic tables and campfires, and playing cards in the camper. My mom and stepdad even rediscovered their musical talents, and they spent hours playing and singing on special keyboards that were, as we would say, "travable."

It was such a joy to see this family being rewarded with happiness, after all the members had endured times of heartache. So wonderful to know that God was aware of the difficult paths we were traveling, and He was guiding them to cross at just the right time. It is impossible to think of those happy times with my "papa" without a smile.

Dedicated to Alvie Doyle Tuggle,
August 17, 1921 to July 5, 2004.

Behavior as Becometh Holiness (Titus 2:3)

"A time to weep and a time to laugh; a time to mourn, and a time to dance" (Ecclesiastes 3:4). All of those times happened in one week as we bid goodbye to the matriarch of the Carlisle family, Ida Mae Weaver Carlisle, age 82.

A funeral is the ultimate reality check for a family. Many of us learned about bereavement policies. At one company "grandmother-in-law" did not qualify for paid time off, and at another "close friend of the family" did. The airlines don't have a discount for this purpose anymore.

We were reminded of the strength of our support groups. Families, friends, neighbors, and churches all showed their true colors, stepping up to comfort while providing all of our needs.

Of course, there was weeping and mourning, but also laughing as we recalled the sweet and wonderful Mama, Grandma, Aunt, and sister that was Ida Mae. As for the dancing: a favorite CD by our friends, the Heavenly Echoes, provided upbeat, inspirational songs that could not be listened to without tapping a toe or swaying to the rhythm. We also were reminded of our own strength as we were able to write, speak, and sing to honor her at the service.

I couldn't have loved her more if she'd been my own mama, instead of my husband's. Though she was a full six inches shorter, I looked up to her. She seemed to be cut straight out of the second chapter of Titus, where the writer advises women to be discreet, chaste, keepers at home.

Anyone who knew this wonderful lady knows that she used the Bible as her blueprint, and gave us a perfect pattern to follow.

Our minister described her as uncomplicated, and many of her interests would not surprise you at all. She loved quilting and cooking. She had a way with flowers, both in the yard and in her windowsill. The special voice she employed to talk to a favorite dog or one of her many cats will stick in our minds forever. Looking out her window, she loved to watch birds at a feeder, especially the redbirds.

Unless you engaged her in conversation, you might not be aware of her interest in politics and sports. She was a classic yellow dog Democrat, and a concerned and interested member of her community. During sporting events when the Hogs weren't playing, she would pull for any Arkansas team, or any Texas team. From Little League to pros, football, basketball, or baseball, she'd be tuned in and cheering.

Many may remember her mostly for what she didn't do. She never worked outside the home; she knew how to drive, but chose not to; she didn't drink or party. She didn't gossip or speak ill of anyone. Even the most despicable newsmakers drew this comment: "I love his soul, but I hate what he did."

She was a member of a team. For sixty years, she wanted to be beside her husband as much as possible. At the dinner table, in front of the TV, in the church pew, on his delivery trips across Arkansas. Though he was the boss, she'd remind him of the rules of the road with snapping fingers and stern looks.

Her favorite Book also reminds us that "by their fruits ye shall know them" (Matthew 7:20). Those who attended her service at Ashby's could see those fruits plainly. A strong, close family, loving friends, a congregation of young women striving to follow her example. She also taught us never to take anything in this life for granted. She knew the real treasures were stored in Heaven. To borrow one of her favorite phrases: "Lord willin'", we'll see her there someday.

Dedicated to Ida Mae Weaver Carlisle,
January 29, 1926 to February 4, 2008.

"It's Not Who You Knew, and It's Not What You Did…"

"…It's how you lived." These words come from a song made popular by a Ouachita-born singing group, Point of Grace. There's so much truth here. Only a few of us will ever invent something so valuable that our name is remembered. Some will be associated with a famous person; a smattering will have more than our own fifteen-minute share of fame. So how will we be remembered?

My husband's father would not be considered famous by any stretch of the definition of that word. But, well-known, well-respected, well thought of? Of course. How does a person with a seemingly ordinary life accomplish this? It's how you live.

As a young man, he established a reputation. He was the tall, smiling one with a full head of hair and James-Deanish good looks. His friends and younger relatives knew he was always up for an adventure, willing to do anything to help someone else. Not reckless, just fearless. If it needed doing, R.V. would do it.

In his work life, this tendency grew. As a timber worker, he was one of the biggest, strongest, and hardest-working men any employer could hope for. Foul weather, injuries, lack of food or water, no worries. He just kept going till the job was finished.

During his career as a delivery truck driver, he became known for taking what was needed from one point to the other with no complaints. He was the one who could get the truck in and out of impossible spots, up roads that couldn't even really be called that. His customers were glad to see him coming, and often rewarded him with home-baked treats and friendly conversation. On longer trips, his wife accompanied him, making sure he followed all the rules of the road. Once more, no complaints. He truly enjoyed her company.

His family and friends know all of this because he loved to talk about it. His stories included minute details that most of us would discard as unimportant. To R.V., every measurement, ever price he paid, every date and time was part of the rich fabric of his life. No event was too small to make a good tale.

Sixty years of steady companionship with the love of his life created a pattern that all who knew them still strive to follow. They made it look easy, and paraphrasing a verse from the book of Romans (12:10), they were kindly affectioned and honorably preferred each other.

His children and grandchildren looked up (literally) to him as a firm, reliable example of a Christian father. He never criticized, but often richly praised their accomplishments. For concerts, contests, and award ceremonies, he was in the front row, with a huge, proud smile. "That's my boy (or girl)" was written all over his face, displayed on his wall, and even on the bumper of his truck. He was the first one they called with good news, because they knew he'd love hearing it.

As a member of the community and leader at his church, he could be depended on for whatever was required. During the construction of his congregation's new building, the members purchased a set of tires for his truck. He had literally burned up the road going back and forth to bring the necessary supplies. His caring attention to detail shows in the fine facility they still call home.

Some men have a hard time communicating. On the contrary, R.V. loved to talk, and loved to listen. He wanted to be up-to-date on the happenings in your life, and shared every detail of his. We expected to talk to him every day, and more than once on football game days. His "how 'bout them Hawgs (or Hornets)" phone calls are legendary in our family.

So, when the last chapter of your story is written, how will others remember you? That dash between beginning and end dates on your headstone will tell it all. It's how you lived.

Dedicated with love to R.V. Carlisle,
October 29, 1925 to October 4, 2009.

Streetcars and Ravens: Lessons from Mama

"Men are like streetcars: if you don't catch this one, there will be another along very shortly." And, "Don't mock your mother; the ravens will peck out your eyes." Unorthodox? Maybe even a little disturbing? For me, these two pieces of advice rank right up there with "Always wear clean underwear, in case you are in an accident." The oft-repeated admonitions I heard over the years reveal a lot about who my mother really was.

My mama spent her early years in the San Francisco, California, area. Thus, the streetcar reference. Really, it's not like there were multiple men in her life. She married my daddy when she was seventeen, they divorced, and she raised me and my sister as a single mother. Then, she married the love of her life when she was forty. I think this unusual gem had been spoken by her own mother, and its message is a good one for young women. They mean to say to us, don't pin your hopes, your dreams, your life on another person. Be stable enough in yourself that you can carry on. Thankfully, I have not had to test this in my own lifetime.

The second, rather graphic, reference also came via my grandmother. She was sent to a convent (what we would term today as a private school) as a youngster. I didn't realize the origin of this "threat" until I saw the movie *The Passion of the Christ*. An unforgettable image, to be sure. Always delivered tongue-in-cheek, it usually followed something a bit embarrassing or funny that had happened to Granny or

Mama. It was meant to remind us to be respectful (while hiding our giggles behind our hands.)

"Get mad at it, and get it done", usually followed by my full name, Jenny Sue. A natural-born procrastinator and conflict avoider, it has always taken more than a little prompting to get me up and moving. This particular one always pops into my head as deadlines approach, or when the kitchen needs cleaning after a family dinner.

"There's a lot of great free stuff to do out there." As children, she took us on a vacation every year, and we stretched those dollars until they squealed. We traveled to California once in a VW bug, and though we didn't camp out (recall the single parent thing), we did cook out on a Coleman camp stove at rest areas along the way. Some attractions were pretty pricey at times, but we also entered every museum, read every historical marker, and stood on the curb for every parade we could find. What great memories!

"Enjoy God's creation, but don't be afraid to grab a hoe or a shovel to whack something when necessary." Okay, these actual words never crossed her lips. But there was a contrast that speaks volumes in my mother's life. She loved to stand at her kitchen window to watch the birds that built their nest in the artificial flowers in the window box. However, when her faithful dog awakened the neighborhood by barking incessantly at an invading critter, she would venture out, armed with a flashlight and the sharpest garden implement she could find to dispatch the varmint, whether it was an opossum, or even a poisonous snake. This was one reason we encouraged her to wear an alert button as she got older.

"Be creative." Another one I learned by her example. She was an expert at brightening every corner where she lived, and on a budget. Seasonal decorations, homemade Christmas ornaments, hand-painted craft items that sold like hotcakes when she and my stepdad were "on the road." There was no limit to her imagination and her desire to share it.

"Be generous, even if you have to be sneaky about it." With apologies to our frugal husbands. Mama was all about slipping some cash to you discreetly, and she had a list of charities that were the beneficiaries of what she called "drops in the bucket" each month. I'm sure they are all missing her dependability very much these days.

"The perfect place to learn to sing harmony is inside a VW bug." What wonderful songs emerged as we bounced along. Everything we heard at church or on the radio was fair game. If you rode along with us, joining in was a survival technique.

"Find out all you can about your ancestors." Books, books, and more books survive to be distributed to her children, stepchildren, grandchildren. It's all there. The answer to every question you could ever pose. She would always remind you to look it up in your family book. Goodness knows, she spent enough time compiling them!

"Make friends everywhere you go." This is probably her most surprising legacy. There was not a doctor visit, a trip to the grocery store, or a walk to the mailbox that didn't include smiling and speaking to someone, especially those who looked a little downtrodden. A quick honk on the bicycle horn attached to her walking stick broke the ice, and pleasant conversation always followed. As her time on earth ran out, we were amazed at the people that literally came out of the woodwork to bid her Godspeed. She had friends she talked to on the phone, corresponded with by mail, hugged on her way down the hall at the nursing home. These were not just token gestures of respect, but true and lasting friendships. Try as I might, I feel I will never measure up to her success in this regard. But I owe it to her to keep trying.

So, for the first time in my life, I have no one to send a Mother's Day card to. I can only hope that my legacy will be as interesting and inspirational.

This column is dedicated with all my love to
Merry Lu Barnett McLeod Tuggle,
November 22, 1933 to November 1, 2013.

The Family Headquarters

From the street, it looks like an ordinary, forty-year-old mobile home with a house roof, a large porch, and a rock foundation. The uninformed observer would not suspect the details that make this location a treasure trove of great stories.

Just behind the double gate that leads to the back yard is a very small fence that is completely useless, but at the same time legendary. Once a connector between the old gate and the side of the house, it stands four feet tall and less than two feet wide, with a metal post firmly set in concrete on each side. A friend who is a consummate story-teller remembers this piece of chain link each time he sees any member of our family. What sort of dog, he wonders, would be small enough to stand behind the fence, and well trained enough to stay there, without any means of containment? More entertaining than any story this likable guy could tell is the enjoyment he gets out of that silly fence.

In the front yard, a very large flower bed constructed from railroad ties holds white rock, a flagpole, and a soda parlor-style chair made of painted iron reinforcement bar. Decorated with artificial flowers at the beginning of each season, the whole thing conceals a massive stump that marks the spot where a huge pine tree once stood. The flag flies proudly, and along with a yellow ribbon tied to a nearby tree, it portrays the love of country that lived in the heart of the latest occupant of the house. At various times over the years, this display was accompanied by large signs stating displeasure over the way the government was handling current affairs. On the porch, a lighted cross burned 24/7, leaving no doubt about the priorities of the family.

Inside the fence that goes all the way around the yard, canines of all shapes and sizes have chased squirrels and provided a noisy welcome to all who ventured in. A very fertile garden spot in the back corner is now their final resting place.

Three sheds occupy the lot. One was a fully equipped workshop, where all manner of crafts, furniture, scout projects, and science fair entries were constructed. A wood-burning stove, numerous bright lights, and a front and back door that enabled a wonderful breeze made this a comfortable hangout for residents of the male persuasion. When something in the house needed fixing, whatever was required could be easily located here. A second shed made of fiberglass panels housed the family's clothes dryer. Located here as a safety consideration, its distance from the washing machine in the kitchen made for some exciting back and forth trips on bad weather days. The third building is larger and sturdier than many homes, and housed shelves full of seasonal items, from Christmas decorations to ice chests and camp stoves.

Inside, the memories speak with a clearer voice. The layout has always seemed a little more spacious than a single-wide mobile home, and the addition of a family room with a rock hearth along one side makes it truly unique and welcoming. The wide opening into the room was graced with a ramp at one time, when the owner used a motorized scooter to travel around. More than just a convenience, this became a built-in amusement park ride for great-grandchildren. That same room became an oversized bedroom when the family living there outgrew the designated spaces on each end of the house. Heated for most of the years with a wood-burning stove, many warm and happy voices still echo from the wood-paneled walls.

Everywhere you look are improvements added by different members of the family. The son-in-law who had a day job in a synthetic marble plant practiced his trade in the kitchen and both bathrooms over the years. One daughter added phone jacks, and some rowdy grandsons once left a dent in the bedroom door.

The dining area window has had a bird feeder within view, and it provides a perfect point to contemplate that spacious yard and the buffer of trees behind it. Somewhere beyond the back fence are more houses, but they are far enough away that you get a good sense of country living with your bacon and eggs each day. Over the kitchen sink, another window has view of a flower box that has been a favorite nesting place for feathered friends. Better than any televised nature program, anyone who remained quiet long enough could witness tiny lives beginning in an up-close and-personal fashion.

At some point in the not-so-distant future, this property will change hands. Children who grew up here have families of their own. The handy men that repaired it have their own homes to maintain. Hopefully, another family will move in and make new memories. For one patched-together bunch of kids, grands and great-grands, this place has served its purpose many times over, and will live in our hearts forever.

Relaunching to Whatever Comes Next

The sixties. A time of westerns and cartoons on television. A time for playing hide-and-go-seek, kick-the-can, Cowboys and Indians. A time for wearing dresses, bobby socks, and saddle oxfords to school every day. A great time to grow up for sure. But, now, I am in *my* sixties. That's a different concept all together.

It's a time to look back and be amazed at all I have seen. To realize that my first memory of watching live TV was President Kennedy's funeral. To remember sitting in the dining hall of Camp Mintahama watching the first man on the moon on a tiny, grainy, black-and-white TV with a whole room of normally rowdy Girl Scouts, yet you could have literally heard a pin drop. To appreciate how well God has things figured out to bring my little three-person family from Kansas to Arkansas at just the right time for our future to unfold.

The feeling I have was illustrated well when I was sitting on a beach with my husband this past winter. How amazing to be on an island in the Bahamas, with the man of my dreams. Far from everything familiar. Enjoying the most incredibly beautiful colors and scenery ever. To know that we were there because our children had collected money for an anniversary present to send us on a cruise. To watch the amazing, frightening power of God as He sent little rain clouds around us, gentle waves lapping on the beach, a small but mighty boat to take us back to the safety of the cruise ship.

Here I am, Lord. Send me. I am ready for whatever You

have in mind. You have blessed me beyond measure. I can trust You completely. If I can only keep myself from second guessing You, and just get out of the way.

I am Yours.

ABOUT THE AUTHOR

Jenny McLeod Carlisle has been writing stories since she learned to hold a pencil. Her first seventeen years were spent in Southeast Kansas, where she grew up with her divorced mom and younger sister in a very happy and busy home. Writing letters to her daddy helped develop her "voice."

After moving to Arkansas just before graduating from high school, she married the love of her life and settled in as a career State of Arkansas employee. They now have three married children and six grandchildren who are living very successful lives in Arkansas, Florida, and Texas.

Along the way, Jenny became a columnist for the monthly magazine *Ouachita Life*, which is widely distributed in the southwest quadrant of the state. She loves hearing from her readers, and wishes them God's richest blessings as they travel the road He has set out for them.